THE TORNADO SCIENTIST

SCIENTIST

Seeing Inside Severe Storms

MARY KAY CARSON

WITH PHOTOGRAPHS BY

TOM UHLMAN

Houghton Mifflin Harcourt

Boston   New York

The text type was set in Proxima Nova.
The display type was set in Strobos Std and Directors Gothic 210.

Library of Congress Cataloging-in-Publication Data

Names: Carson, Mary Kay, author. | Uhlman, Tom, illustrator.
Title: The tornado scientist : seeing inside severe storms / Mary Kay Carson
; with photographs by Tom Uhlman.
Description: Boston ; New York : Houghton Mifflin Harcourt, [2019] | Series:
Scientist in the field | Audience: Ages 10–12. | Audience: Grades 4 to 6.
Identifiers: LCCN 2018034811 | ISBN 9780544965829 (hardcover)
Subjects: LCSH: Tanamachi, Robin—Juvenile literature. | Tornadoes—Juvenile
literature. | Storm chasers—Biography—Juvenile literature. |
Meteorologists—Biography—Juvenile literature. | Women
scientists—Biography—Juvenile literature.
Classification: LCC QC955.2 .C364 2019 | DDC 551.55/3—dc23
LC record available at https://lccn.loc.gov/2018034811

ISBN 978-0-544-96582-9

Manufactured in China
SCP 10 9 8 7 6 5 4 3 2 1
4500743906

*Dan Dawson and a colleague carry a PIPS near a radar truck.
It's made to be heavy so it'll stay upright in strong winds.*

CONTENTS

> Robin and her team get the radar truck parked and ready to scan for storms.

This 2007 Texas twister is one of the many tornadoes Robin has seen while storm chasing.

Chapter 1
A Southern Twist

Beep . . . beep . . . beep . . . An odd-looking truck backs up slowly. The vehicle is on a bridge that crosses over a highway. Once safely settled onto the shoulder, the truck stops. But its windshield wipers keep going—slapping away the steady cold rain.

As soon as the beeping backup alarm goes silent, a door swings open. A woman scrambles out, her black hair tossed by the wind and her glasses gathering raindrops. She jogs to the rear of the unusual flatbed truck, pulls the starter rope on a generator, plugs an orange extension cord into it, and sprints for the shelter of the truck cab. Robin Tanamachi is back inside within two minutes. Maybe three.

A whirring noise soon starts up. It's loud enough to hear over the wind and traffic and is coming from the back of the truck. A contraption towers over the cab from its mount on the truck's bed. It looks a bit like a giant mechanical mushroom.

The big white machine slowly swivels as it whirs. *Whhzzzszzzhhh.* It turns toward a group of fast-moving dark clouds off in the distance. The angry-looking patch of sky speeds over an old red barn on its way toward the waiting truck.

This is a mobile radar truck, a vehicle with a radar mounted on its back.

< Robin checks in with the radar map during an Alabama storm chase.

1

Weather scientists, called meteorologists, use mobile radar to track severe weather. Researchers drive radar trucks to a storm so they can scan it up close and see what's going on inside the dark clouds and whipping winds. Radar trucks are how storm-chasing meteorologists study Earth's fastest windstorms—tornadoes.

Outside might be wet and windy, but the inside of the truck looks like a cramped computer lab. Half of the cab is filled with bolted-down electronic equipment. Three humans are stuffed in there, too. Each stares at weather-tracking maps on laptop screens.

The big storms are still pretty far away. And they aren't all that strong—at least not yet. So why aren't these tornado researchers driving toward the storms? What happened to the *chase* in storm chasers?

< Robin and her team get the radar ready to scan the coming storm in Alabama.

AMERICA'S STORMY SPOTS

^ Tornadoes happen in nearly all states east of the Rocky Mountains, but these areas are especially prone to strong twisters.

^ Stormy skies have always fascinated Robin.

THE OTHER TORNADO ALLEY

Robin Tanamachi is a meteorologist, tornado scientist, and radar expert. She is also a veteran storm chaser. She's crisscrossed Tornado Alley from Texas to the Dakotas. Chasing down a storm as it spins out a tornado is pretty much her favorite thing to do. It's why Robin became a scientist. But today's tornado hunt is different.

Her team is hunkered down in the truck, waiting for the storms to come to them. It's not the safest setup. If a tornado suddenly drops out of the sky, it'll take a while to shut down the radar and drive away. They're sitting ducks.

A big pickup slows to a stop alongside the radar truck. Robin rolls down her window. The pickup driver wears a ball cap and friendly smile.

"Y'all need help?" he asks in a southern drawl as thick as country ham.

This isn't Kansas, or any of the Great Plains states of Tornado Alley. It's the American South. Alabama, to be exact. Southern states like Alabama, Georgia, and Tennessee might not be the first places you'd name when thinking about dangerous tornadoes. But they should be.

Twisters kill more people down South than in the Great Plains. Why does the so-called Dixie Alley region have such deadly tornadoes? "The laws of physics aren't different here," says Robin.

Tornado chasing can be dangerous, but it's how scientists collect information on these short-lived storms.

^ Tornado winds are powerful enough to bend metal, rip off roofs, and topple trees.

4

"Water still evaporates at 212°F [100°C] degrees." Gravity pulls rain down toward the ground the same way in both Tennessee and Texas. But the two twister alleys aren't identical. Some of those differences are weather related, but not all.

Part of the devastation brought about by these southern storms has little to do with weather science or meteorology. A tornado doesn't harm anyone if no one lives in its path. Lots of people live in the South, nearly twice as many as in the Midwest. Many southern homes are less sturdy, too.

Mobile home communities are more common where winters are mild.

Twisters in the South are also harder to see and track among the hills, valleys, and forests of Dixie Alley. Southern tornadoes often happen with little warning and are more likely to spin out at night. All this works against storm-chasing tornado scientists trying to learn about these dangerous storms. Researchers can't improve tornado forecasting methods that might save lives without studying the storms.

Instead of chasing severe storms, researchers studying Dixie Alley twisters go for the ambush. They set up weather instruments in what they estimate is the storm's path and hope a tornado happens. It's like setting a net and waiting for a huge spinning tube of air to get caught in it.

At least that's the plan. Robin and her radar truck team are part of a group of scientists trying to better understand southern tornadoes. The project is called VORTEX Southeast. Its mission? Saving lives through science and educating the public on how to stay safe.

> The day after a tornado, a homeowner looks at what's left.

^ This family survived unharmed when their home was struck by a tornado.

By studying the conditions, timing, and strength of Dixie Alley's most dangerous storms, they hope to help communities create better warning systems. The people in charge of keeping residents safe need facts.

Rainy-day storm chases. Noisy radar trucks. Science teamwork. It's all part of being a tornado scientist.

And that's all Robin Tanamachi has ever wanted to be.

Chapter 2
Storm Chaser Genesis

"Robin! Come and see what's on TV!" One late afternoon on a hot summer day in 1986, seven-year-old Robin was at home in Minnesota. Her dad was watching the local news.

"Robin!" he called. "Get a load of this!"

What looked like a gigantic funnel of white cotton candy spun in a forest of evergreen trees. The video was coming in live from a news helicopter. It was a tornado spinning through a local park!

Robin watched as the tornado plowed over power lines, sending up flashes of sparks and exploding flames. The tornado yanked one-hundred-year-old trees out of the ground like weeds and shredded them into wood chips.

"It was the coolest thing I'd ever seen," Robin remembers. It was a real-time tornado chase on live TV.

News stations replayed the rare video for days. It was the first ever live broadcast of a tornado from start to finish. Robin got to see it again and again. (This was before YouTube.) Young Robin soaked it all up, including TV interviews with meteorologists from a place called the National Severe Storms Lab (NSSL).

"That was how I found out that there were scientists who studied storms for a living," says Robin. "And it sounded like the coolest job in the world." She got a look at storm-chasing scientists in action soon after on the famous "Tornado!" episode of the television show *NOVA*.

Robin had seen her future. "I knew I wanted to be a research meteorologist studying severe weather," she says.

Robin calls the 1986 Brooklyn Park, Minnesota, tornado "my gateway tornado." It's what got her hooked.

GEIGER COUNTERS AND CAREER DAY

A second-grader deciding to be a research meteorologist might seem unusual. But not for Robin. "I was always interested in weather—from the beginning," explains Robin. She can't remember a time when she didn't want to know how things worked in the natural world.

Robin's parents encouraged her and her younger sister (who's also a scientist) to explore whatever interested them.

Finding helpful books was easy. Their mother was a librarian.

"My dad was an electrical engineer," says Robin. He had a basement lab with computers, a microscope, and electrical equipment he let his daughters play with. It seemed normal growing up, but Robin now realizes it was unusual. "Not every kid gets to play with a Geiger counter or microscope at home."

By the time she was in high school in the mid-1990s, Robin was a known weather nerd. When her art class made

a mural of the town's history, "I was charged with painting the panel about the tornado that struck the town in 1981."

The self-described "flannel-clad tornado geek" even got to meet a real National Weather Service meteorologist during a high school career day. When she brought up tornadoes, the meteorologist advised her to study lots of math and physics. And he told Robin about a tornado video series. "It's how I got my tornado video fix for the next several years," says Robin.

ᵛ Seven-year-old Robin checks out a rocky creek. Her family went on lots of nature walks.

ᵛ Second-grader Robin shows off her science fair project on rainbows.

ᵛ By third grade, Robin was a certified bookworm.

THE CHASING LIFE

Robin finally got to see a real live tornado during college. She and other meteorology students took a severe weather field trip out in Tornado Alley one summer.

"I got to see the waving fields of wheat and experience eating gas-station burritos," says Robin. She loved "being in the wide open plains where you can see fifty miles [80 km] in every direction."

The giant thunderhead clouds and rotating supercell storms she'd learned about in books and classrooms were right there in front of her. It was all real.

"We actually didn't see any tornadoes that week," says Robin. "But I got hooked on the lifestyle of chasing." The fun of road trips, the excitement of the hunt, and the camaraderie of storm chasers spoke to her.

Luckily, the students went chasing locally the following week near Benson, Minnesota. And that's where Robin Tanamachi saw her first twister. "It didn't matter that it was really skinny and wasn't a very remarkable tornado," says Robin. "It was okay that it was only an F1. It was *my* first tornado!"

During her last year of college, Robin asked a professor about going on to study meteorology in graduate school. She knew that graduate school was the next step in becoming a research scientist.

Glancing at her grades, he told Robin to forget it. The professor said that her one C meant she wasn't cut out for graduate school. Robin believed him. After all, wasn't it his job to know which students could become research meteorologists?

^ High-schooler Robin in front of the mural panel she painted featuring the 1981 Roseville, Minnesota, tornado.

< Middle-school-aged Robin looks out over Spirit Lake. The dead trees floating on the water were killed by the eruption of nearby Mount St. Helens. The volcano exploded in 1980.

THE PLAINS TRUTH

After graduation, Robin went to work operating meteorology equipment for research scientists. The job took her back to Tornado Alley with a research team for a week. "While there I got to experience some storms," remembers Robin. "I realized I really loved severe weather." The drama, excitement, and power of a sky full of wind and lightning still called to her.

After a year on the job, Robin's bosses asked if she wanted to become a research meteorologist. She explained that she'd been told by a professor that she wasn't good enough. Don't listen to him, they said, you clearly have what it takes. If she wanted to go to graduate school, they'd write letters recommending her.

Robin filled out and sent in applications to four different schools. Every single one accepted her. A ringing telephone made the choice easy. "Howie Bluestein called me up," says Robin. She recognized the famous storm chaser from the *NOVA* "Tornado!" show. Howie Bluestein isn't just a tornado celebrity. He's also a research scientist and professor at the University of Oklahoma.

Dr. Bluestein asked Robin if she wanted to come study tornadoes with him. Uh, yeah. "I packed everything I owned into a U-Haul and I drove down to Oklahoma," says Robin. Oklahoma and tornadoes go together like biscuits and gravy. It's home to the NSSL and ground zero for Tornado Alley action.

During her thirteen years in Oklahoma, Robin would chase some of the world's fastest, biggest, and most destructive tornadoes ever. And live to tell about it.

ᵛ Robin saw a lot of big storms while studying in Oklahoma and chasing in Tornado Alley. She photographed this picture-perfect Texas supercell thunderstorm in 2011.

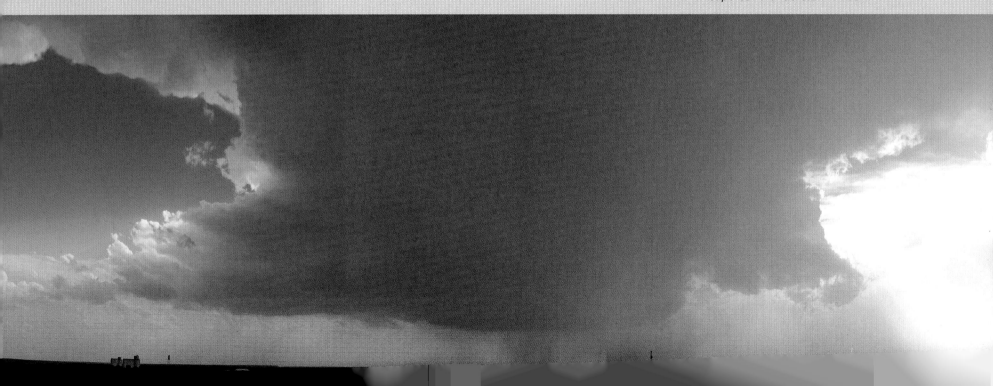

TYPHOON CHASER

^ Robin visiting Japan.

Tornadoes aren't the only storms worth chasing. Hurricanes are gigantic sea storms. In Asia they are called typhoons. When Robin got the chance to spend three months in Japan chasing typhoons, she grabbed it. What young meteorologist would pass up seeing such enormous storms up close? Getting to visit Japan was another reason to take the job.

"My last name is Tanamachi," says Robin. "I'm fourth generation Japanese American." She speaks *sukoshi* Japanese. (*Sukoshi* means "a little" or "some.") But Robin had never been to Japan before. This was her chance.

Between chasing typhoons, Robin traveled to Fukuoka, where her father's relatives live. Everyone treated her like close family, calling her their American cousin.

"When I left to go back to Tokyo they all came down to the bus station to wave goodbye," remembers Robin. "I was very touched by that." Typhoon science wasn't the only research Robin got to do during her time in Japan. She learned about family history, too.

Robin taking in the city sights of Osaka, Japan.

6:29
6:32 6:31 6:35
6:33 6:36
6:27 6:37 6:38 6:41
6:42

6:26

6:25
6:04
6:05 6:24
6:06
6:07 6:23
6:08 6:22
6:09 6:21
6:10 6:15 6:16 6:20
6:11 6:12 6:17
6:14 6:18 6:19
6:13

The El Reno tornado was so powerful that it left a scar on the landscape so big that it showed up on satellite images taken from more than 22,000 miles (35,700 km) out in space. The white-shaded area shows the extent of destruction surrounding the pink path marked with times of passage.

N

The El Reno tornado was the widest twister ever recorded. At one point, it was 2.5 miles (4 km) wide and armed with winds spinning at 295 miles (475 km) per hour. That's the second fastest on record.

This is the storm that spawned the El Reno twister.

The El Reno tornado killed four veteran storm chasers, including Tim Samaras and Richard Henderson, who died in this vehicle.

Chapter 3
Twister Science 2.0

"Look at that!" Dan Dawson is a fellow storm-chasing meteorologist and Robin's husband. In a YouTube video, Dan is yelling and looking toward the golden grassy field on the other side of the country road. He spots a tornado.

About a mile away, a dark, funnel-shaped windstorm twists and spins. Even at that distance, there's no doubt. It's a tornado. This is flat-as-a-pancake Oklahoma, after all. The sky is big and the horizon is always out there.

The twister seems extra wide. Dan stares at the storm. Are there actually two tornadoes? Or is it three? Four?

"Multiple vortex tornado!" Dan yells over the wind. A bolt of lightning adds an exclamation point. Everyone near the parked car scrambles to photograph and video the impressive tornado. But Dan and Robin both realize something is wrong. The huge tornado had switched direction.

"It's coming toward us! We gotta go!" says Dan.

"Back in the car, everybody," Robin says from the driver's seat. "Now!"

Both back doors slam as passengers slide in. Dan is already buckled in and riding shotgun next to Robin.

"Drive, Robin! Go, go, GO!" says Dan. "Seriously, we're in trouble." Robin pulls the car onto the pavement and heads out.

"Robin, it's *right behind us! GO!*" says Dan.

^ This picture is from the video Robin shot before fleeing the El Reno tornado. How many funnel-shaped vortices do you see?

14

But Robin couldn't go any faster. There was a traffic jam of storm-chaser vehicles running from the tornado. Robin decided not to look back. She needed to focus on driving. Only on driving.

"I tuned out everything else," Robin later wrote in her blog. "I had to keep my head, and keep the car on the road."

Car accidents kill more chasers than the storms. Robin knows that. Inside the car were two friends, her husband, and her unborn first son.

"I was seven months pregnant at the time," Robin says. So, she just drove.

The car windows and doors whistled from wild winds trying to get in. "I felt my ears start to pop," she wrote on her blog. "The pickup in front of me began to fishtail." She got ready to swerve out of its way, but the driver pulled out of the slide.

Then it was over. The giant twister lifted off to the north. Robin, Dan, their baby, and their friends were okay.

That "chase was my only one in which I was actually afraid of being overtaken and possibly killed by a tornado," Robin blogged. She credits cautiousness for their "escape unscathed from the claws of a murderous, multi-vortex EF-5 [tornado]."

Others weren't as lucky. The Oklahoma El Reno tornado killed eight people and injured more than one hundred on May 31, 2013. The National Weather Service called it "the most dangerous tornado in storm observing history."

STORMY SCIENCE

What causes dangerous tornadoes like the 2013 one in El Reno, Oklahoma? Why do some thunderstorms produce tornadoes while others don't? What makes the winds in an existing storm spin into a tornado?

Scientists created VORTEX to find out. The first Verification of the Origins of Rotation in Tornadoes Experiment (VORTEX) project happened in 1994 and 1995. VORTEX2 took tornado research to the next level.

VORTEX2 was the largest tornado research project in history. For five weeks during the spring of 2009 and 2010 more than one hundred scientists chased storms across Tornado Alley from

^ VORTEX2 ran down this Wyoming tornado in 2009.

VORTEX2 scientists scanned and studied supercell storms, including this one.

Texas to southern Minnesota. Robin was one of them.

"We were a fully nomadic band of about forty vehicles," says Robin. A caravan of that many trucks and cars roving through rural towns is hard to miss. "We turned heads."

Ten mobile radars were among the VORTEX2 vehicles. Their job? To continually scan the skies to identify twister-making storms. Once tornado-producing storms were spotted, the science teams drove to them and deployed all kinds of weather instruments:

Ten mobile radar trucks participated in VORTEX2.

remote-controlled drones, weather balloons, extra-tough weather instrument packages, and video recorders.

A lot of what meteorologists know today about tornadoes is thanks to the VORTEX2 program. For the first time, their instruments measured and recorded a storm creating a tornado during its whole life cycle.

That's right. A tornado has a life cycle. A storm gives birth to it, the tornado grows, and then it dies. The storm that creates the tornado has a life cycle, too.

"You can think of a storm as an organism," explains Robin. Like living things, a tornado needs food to grow and strengthen. And it dies when its energy is used up.

A tornado happens when a thunderstorm releases some of its energy. But not every thunderstorm whips up a tornado. In fact, most don't. Tornadoes are rare even though thunderstorms are common.

At this very moment on Earth about two thousand storms are booming thunder, flashing lightning, and dumping rain. Thunderstorms are ordinary events. They happen whenever and wherever warm air full of water vapor rises up into a ceiling of cold air.

17

You probably know that warm air rises and cold air sinks. Why? Cold air is heavier, thanks to its more tightly packed, slow-moving molecules. When warm moist air rises up into cold air, the moist air cools and the water vapor turns into drops of liquid, or condenses. Just like dew on grass or fog on your glasses. The rising moist air is cooler, but still warmer than what's around it, so it keeps on rising.

The warm air continues to rise until it hits the tropopause, which acts like a lid on a pot. Blocked by this lid in the atmosphere, explains Robin, the cloud-making air spreads out horizontally. It creates those flat-topped, anvil-shaped clouds that define a towering thunderhead.

What goes up must come down," says Robin. Some of the air blocked from rising goes in the opposite direction. It sinks. When the sinking air gets rewarmed, it goes back to rising.

It's called a convection cell, a doughnut-shaped loop of air that rises as it warms, sinks as it cools, rises as it warms, etc. Convection cells make clouds. The rising moisture condenses out into floating droplets of water. If there's a lot of warm rising moist air, a thunderhead cloud forms until, boom! You've got a storm.

"A storm is like an engine where the warm moist air is the fuel and the cold dry air that comes out afterward is the exhaust," says Robin. Have you ever stepped outside after a storm and felt how cool it is? "It's because of all the evaporation that's happened." It sucked the heat out of the air.

Sometimes a bunch of convection cells line up like train cars, creating multicell thunderstorms. These can bring severe weather along front lines hundreds of miles long. A front is where two different air masses meet and battle it out in the atmosphere.

^ A late-afternoon developing thunderstorm.

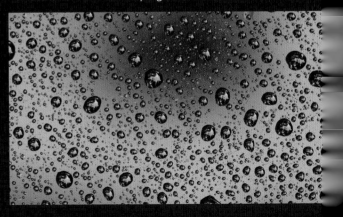

^ The water drops that collect on drinks and steamy bathroom windows come from water vapor in the air condensing on cooler surfaces.

FROM CLOUD TO STORM

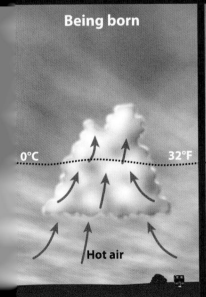

Being born

0°C .... 32°F

Hot air

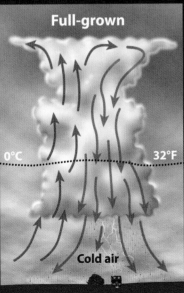

Full-grown

0°C .... 32°F

Cold air

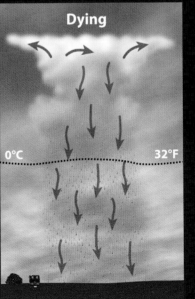

Dying

0°C .... 32°F

And then there are supercells. A supercell is a single-cell monster of a thunderstorm. Gigantic and long-lived, the convection loop inside them pulls air in and up at hurricane wind speeds. Their clouds can reach 8 or more miles (13 km) up into the atmosphere and the storm can grow to be 10 miles (16 km) across, too. And supercells rotate. The whole huge dark blob slowly spins as it hovers overhead like an alien spacecraft that darkens the sky.

Supercells are the serious twister makers. They are powered by an upright tube of air, a mesocyclone, that spirals up into the storm. What make a mesocyclone? Wind shear. Storms can't create tornadoes without it.

Wind shear is wind difference. It happens when winds up high in the atmosphere aren't the same as winds down below. How are they different? The winds in one level are faster or going in a different direction than the winds in the other level.

Mismatched speed, direction, or both is what creates wind shear. Like hands making a clay snake, the differing winds roll the air between them into a tube or cylinder. As the storm keeps growing, powerful winds tip the cylinder upright into a mesocyclone.

With its mesocyclone engine spinning, the supercell gathers fuel by pulling in more warm, moist air up into the storm. This updraft of moist air beneath the rotating mesocyclone creates a low, dark, hanging wall cloud (see photo on p. 23). When a small column of air within the mesocyclone tightens and speeds up, like a spinning ice skater, a funnel cloud drops down from the wall cloud. If the right kind of downdraft pulls the rotating funnel cloud down to the ground, you've got a tornado.

At least that's the basic idea. "It's complicated," admits Robin. Tornado formation, or tornadogenesis, isn't totally understood by meteorologists. Especially the last tornado-triggering bit. What makes a part of the mesocyclone spin up a funnel and then push it down out of the wall cloud? Something has to yank it to the ground. The leading suspect is something called the rear flank downdraft. This powerful downward burst of wind lassoes the air between the wall cloud and the ground, squeezing the already rotating air into a spinning funnel.

TORNADO ANATOMY

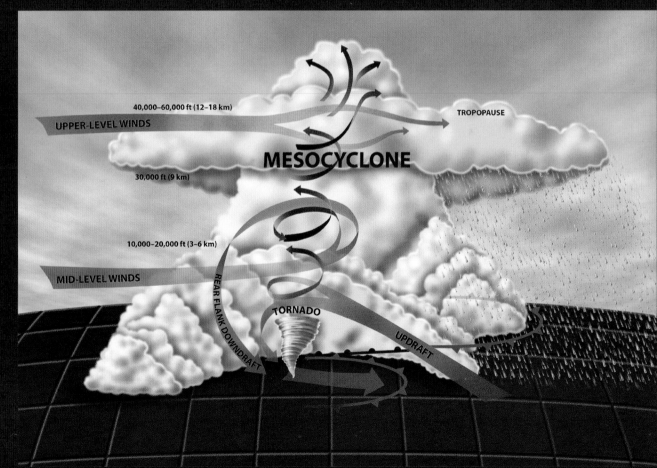

40,000–60,000 ft (12–18 km)

UPPER-LEVEL WINDS

TROPOPAUSE

MESOCYCLONE

30,000 ft (9 km)

10,000–20,000 ft (3–6 km)

MID-LEVEL WINDS

REAR FLANK DOWNDRAFT

TORNADO

UPDRAFT

SUPERCELL SPAWN

Tornadoes are a big deal for houses and cars. But for a miles-wide supercell, a tornado is a small event. "The little tail of a tornado at the bottom of the supercell is maybe five percent of the circulation," explains Robin. The whole storm can reach 8 miles (13 km) up into the atmosphere. That's one and a half Mount Everests.

< Supercells are giant thunderstorms that can grow to be 10 miles (16 km) across.

A tornado is only a tiny part of a supercell. It's a fact that Robin tells people who want to know if a missile could blow up a tornado. "I get that question almost every year," she says. Whatever weapon you could use to blow up a storm 8 miles (13 km) tall would definitely do more damage than any tornado.

^ Many of the VORTEX2 vehicles took a beating driving through hail-dropping storms.

^ The bigger the hailstones, the stronger the storm.

This is why studying the entire life cycle of tornadoes is such a big deal. "It's all updraft at the beginning, and then, it's equal parts updraft and downdraft, and toward the end it's just all downdraft," explains Robin.

Supercells also spit out large hailstones. These frozen balls of ice get caught up in the storm. Updrafts carry them up to the cold heights, where they get an added layer of ice each time they're pulled up through the storm. The stronger the winds inside the supercell, the bigger and heavier the hailstones grow before falling out.

The same part of a supercell that spins out tornadoes dumps hail. Storm chasers know that. Getting hammered by hail while trying to see a twister means you got too close. The storm wasn't moving where you thought it was. Oops.

"Hail damage on a storm chaser's car is a badge of shame," says Robin. "It shows you made a bad forecast."

STORM CHASER SLANG

anvil zits: Frequent lightning within the top spreading portion of a thunderstorm cloud, which is also called an anvil cloud.

blue box: Severe thunderstorm watch.

bust: Severe storm conditions that don't deliver much stormy weather.

clear sky bust: No storms at all, even though severe storm conditions existed.

core punching: Driving through the part of the storm with the heaviest rain and hail—the core. ("Not recommended," says Robin.)

egg beater: Tornado whose condensation funnel isn't touching the ground but has a bunch of surface vortices spinning around it. (Robin's favorite chaser slang word.)

fake-nado: Something that looks like a tornado but isn't.

grunge: Stuff in the air that makes it harder to see a storm, like fog, haze, rain, low clouds, etc.

red box: Tornado watch.

storm chaser: Someone who hunts for and follows storms for research, photography, or news reporting.

storm spotter: On-the-ground volunteer reporter for the National Weather Service.

^ Severe thunderstorms produce lightning as well as the possibility of tornadoes.

A CLOSE CALL

One tornado that caught Robin off guard showered her car with something harder than hail. It happened in Kansas on May 29, 2008, after a long day of storm chasing.

"There was one storm in particular that was producing tornado after tornado," remembers Robin. "And so we just kept following it." Even after the sun set. Chasing storms at night is not only difficult, it's extra dangerous. But the group was on a roll. "We decided to keep chasing as darkness fell," says Robin.

A bolt of lightning lit up the rural landscape for a quick instant. *Flash!* A tornado right next to them!

"I saw this big spinning ring of dirt coming across the field," says Robin. "I realized, oh my gosh, the tornado is right there! And it's coming right for us!"

When the lightning flash faded, it was inky dark again. Where was the tornado now? The driver of the car sped up to get out of the twister's way—or at least to go the direction they thought was away from the tornado.

"That's when it swiped the back end of the vehicle and pelted us with a lot of gravel," says Robin. Yikes! The vehicle following behind Robin's group took a direct hit. No one inside was hurt, but the windows were blown out. The twister pulled a fast one on the storm chasers that night. "It came out from behind two trees and got us." Sometimes you chase the tornado. And sometimes the tornado chases you.

Following the May 29, 2008, Kansas storm as it produced another tornado.

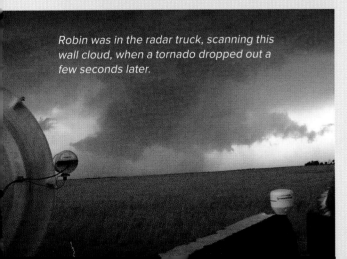

Robin was in the radar truck, scanning this wall cloud, when a tornado dropped out a few seconds later.

RATING TWISTERS

Measuring how fast a tornado is twisting isn't easy. These storms tear up most wind-measuring instruments. Often all that's ever seen of a tornado is the trail of destruction it leaves behind. That's why meteorologists rate tornadoes by the damage done, estimating wind speeds from what was destroyed and what wasn't. Tornadoes are rated from EF-0 to EF-5 on what's called the Enhanced Fujita (EF) Scale. (The name comes from meteorologist Tetsuya Fujita, who developed the scale in the 1970s.)

ENHANCED FUJITA (EF) RATING

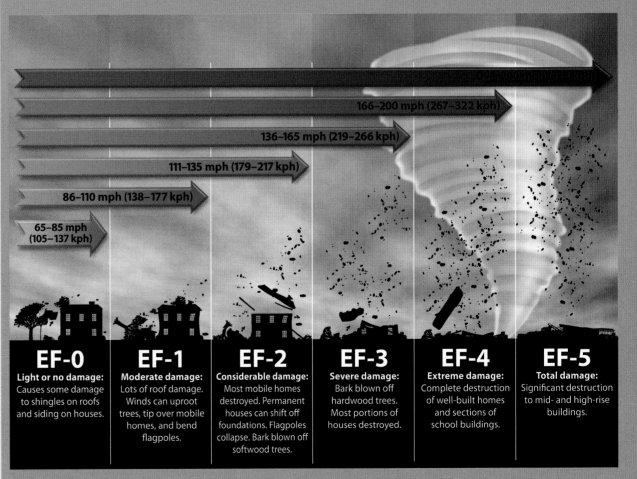

Over 200 mph (322 kph)

166–200 mph (267–322 kph)

136–165 mph (219–266 kph)

111–135 mph (179–217 kph)

86–110 mph (138–177 kph)

65–85 mph (105–137 kph)

EF-0
Light or no damage: Causes some damage to shingles on roofs and siding on houses.

EF-1
Moderate damage: Lots of roof damage. Winds can uproot trees, tip over mobile homes, and bend flagpoles.

EF-2
Considerable damage: Most mobile homes destroyed. Permanent houses can shift off foundations. Flagpoles collapse. Bark blown off softwood trees.

EF-3
Severe damage: Bark blown off hardwood trees. Most portions of houses destroyed.

EF-4
Extreme damage: Complete destruction of well-built homes and sections of school buildings.

EF-5
Total damage: Significant destruction to mid- and high-rise buildings.

Chapter 4
Scanning the Skies

^ This is the weak tornado Robin scanned in Colorado on May 26, 2010, during VORTEX2. No one reported seeing a tornado.

Spotting a tornado at night is tricky. Seeing twisters wrapped by rain or hidden among hills is tough too. Some tornadoes are just harder to see than others. But can a tornado be invisible? Completely unseen by the human eye? Robin Tanamachi thinks so. And she has proof.

In 2010, VORTEX2's roving squadron of storm scientists were storm chasing in western Kansas. On May 25, a weak tornado, only an EF-0, formed under a supercell. The teams successfully studied and scanned the twister. Terrific! Once the show in the sky ended, everyone headed over the Colorado border to a hotel outside of Denver.

The next day, while chasing a nearby storm, the VORTEX2 mobile radars picked up something. The area beneath a supercell looked suspicious. But no one reported seeing a twister.

"One hundred of the best tornado scientists in the world were there watching this storm," says Robin. It lasted eight minutes. "And all of us went home saying there was no tornado."

SCIENCE IT UP

Later on, when Robin took a closer look at the Colorado radar scans, she saw something different. "My radar data shows that there is this feature that looks just like the tornado we saw the day before," Robin says. The Colorado scans were similar to the Kansas tornado radar scans. "Same duration, same kind of wind speeds, but no funnel cloud." Had there been a tornado in Colorado, too?

This is the weak tornado Robin scanned in Kansas on May 25, 2010, during VORTEX2. Everyone agreed it was a tornado.

Robin decided to investigate the question: If it looks like a tornado, lasts as long as a tornado, and behaves like a tornado, *but only on radar*, is it still a tornado?

Robin is a research meteorologist. Research scientists gain knowledge through experiments and observations. Research starts with an idea or explanation for something—a hypothesis. "You design an experiment to test that hypothesis, get your results, and make your conclusions," explains Robin.

Robin's hypothesis? The Colorado tornado was not seen because there wasn't enough moisture in the air to create the foggy part of a funnel cloud.

Robin tested her hypothesis by analyzing the VORTEX2 data. She compared the Kansas and Colorado storms, studying how they were alike and different.

Robin's conclusion? "It was real," says Robin. There had been a tornado in Colorado, too. "It was definitely there." Neither tornado did any damage and no one got hurt. Does it matter if it was a tornado or not?

"As a scientist, I care, " she wrote on her blog. Figuring out what is and what isn't a tornado is important. Just because no one saw it doesn't mean it didn't happen. What humans see is very different from what radar can detect. That's why it's the go-to tool for tornado-tracking meteorologists.

Sometimes a tornado underneath a supercell is obvious—like this one. But twisters aren't always so easy to see.

SURVIVING THE GREENSBURG TORNADO

On May 4, 2007, a half-mile-wide (.8 km) EF-5 wedge tornado plowed through the town of Greensburg, Kansas. It changed the lives of all 1,500 residents. "I was one of them," Megan Gardiner wrote.

The teenager was working at her afterschool restaurant job that evening. The weather had been stormy, but Megan still hoped to meet up with friends later. After going outside to empty the trash around nine thirty p.m. she changed her mind. The lightning was like nothing she'd ever seen. Megan headed home instead.

She joined her family, their dogs, and some neighbors in the home's basement. Megan remembers the local TV weather reporter saying a tornado was headed for Greensburg. Predicted impact was 9:52 p.m. Her phone read 9:47.

^ *Greensburg residents search and sort through what's left of their town.*

We have five minutes, Megan remembered thinking. By now emergency sirens were wailing, winds were howling, and hail as big as golf balls slammed into the house. Then the power went out, leaving everyone in the dark.

"All of a sudden my ears started to pop really bad," remembered Megan. "I mean, this was worse than going in a plane or diving deep under the water." She wrapped herself in a blanket and got ready to crouch down and cover her head. And then it was quiet. Spooky quiet. Until the windows exploded.

"I heard the walls tearing and ripping off into pieces," said Megan. "Then something hit my left shoulder." Chunks of the home were falling onto everyone. And then it was over. It took nearly a half hour to climb out of the basement in the rain and dark.

"We looked back and there was nothing left," wrote Megan. Just piles and piles of rubble. Nearly a thousand homes and buildings were destroyed in Greensburg, Kansas, that night. Eleven people lost their lives in the tornado. Sixty more were injured.

Megan and her family were okay, though the high school senior had nightmares for weeks. That's why she decided to write about what happened. It helped. "But I get very paranoid when a storm comes," admitted Megan.

^ This is what Greensburg, Kansas, looked like after an EF-5 wedge tornado a half mile (.8 km) wide scoured the town in 2007.

^ After a month of hauling away debris from the Greensburg tornado, the town has few remaining buildings.

to see, or detect, objects from a distance. Radar can reveal everything from fighter jets and flocks of birds to valleys at the bottom of the sea.

Weather radar detects precipitation. It picks up all but the tiniest raindrops, hailstones, and snowflakes. Radar does more than locate where this precipitation is falling. It tells you how hard it's coming down, how fast it's moving, and from which direction.

Radar can't see wind directly. Molecules of moving air are too tiny for radar to pick up. But radar can detect whatever the wind moves around—rain, snow, dust, etc.

speed and direction by tracking how fast and where precipitation is being moved by air.

How does weather radar work?

- A magnetron (a) creates microwaves, the same kind of electromagnetic energy that heats up lunch leftovers.
- The radar unit's transmitter sends out quick pulses of microwaves via the antenna (b).
- The microwaves pass through air, but not precipitation. Some of the microwaves hitting water drops (c) scatter in all directions.

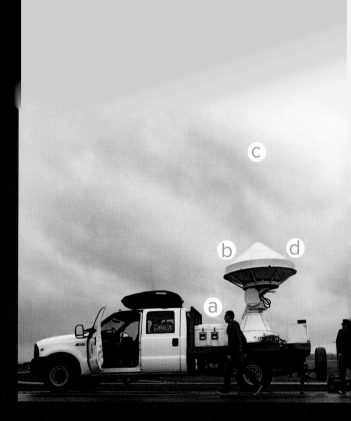

This mobile radar truck from VORTEX2 aims its antenna at a dropping funnel cloud.

A thunderhead cloud spreads into an anvil shape as it hits the tropopause.

- Some of the rain-scattered or snow-scattered microwaves bounce back to the dish-shaped radar. A receiver (d) detects the returned microwaves.

These steps happen fast and continually. The radar emits a pulse, listens for returned signals and records them, and immediately emits another pulse. The entire cycle takes only a millisecond. Fast computers crunch the collected signals instantly, making radar a tool that meteorologists use as weather happens.

Microwaves, like all kinds of electromagnetic energy, travel at the speed of light (186,000 miles [300,000 km] per second). Radar determines the *distance* to a storm by tracking the time it takes for a pulse's echo to bounce back. Knowing the distance along with the direction the transmitter was pointing in tells the radar the exact *location* of the storm. The strength or intensity of the signal returning to the radar depends on what it bounced off of. Echoes

from a rain-dumping thunderstorm are more intense than those from snow flurries. And hailstones bounce back a different kind of signal than sleet.

Computers process all this information into a weather radar map. Like the kind used in TV weather forecasts, the map shows where the storm is and uses colors to identify the kinds and strengths of precipitation it's making.

Most weather radar used in the twenty-first century is called Doppler. This means it not only tracks when echoing signals return but also measures the changes in their frequency. Think of the sound of an ambulance driving past you. Once it's moving away, the siren changes and sounds lower. It changed sound frequency to your ears. Doppler radar uses the changes in microwave frequency to map wind speeds and directions and show which way and how fast a storm is moving.

< One of the 158 National Weather Service high-resolution Doppler weather radars across the United States.

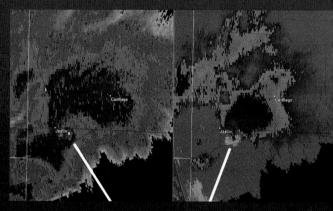

What does a tornado look like on radar? Here are two radar patterns scientists look for: hook echo (bottom) and debris ball (top).

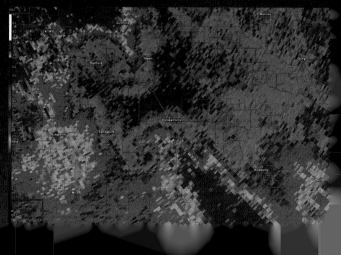

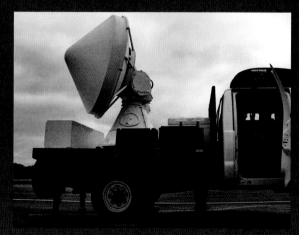

^ These radar antennas can't be aimed, so they emit a wider low-resolution beam.

^ The cone-shaped antenna of this mobile radar is movable. Meteorologists point it toward the section of sky they want to scan.

RADAR EXPERIMENTS

"My job is to come up with an hypothesis about how thunderstorms behave," explained Robin. "And then use instruments like radars and precipitation sensors to test those hypotheses."

Weather radar can locate, measure, and track weather ingredients in the atmosphere. "It's like a Swiss army knife," says Robin. "I'm really interested in opening the hood on severe thunderstorms and figuring out what's going on inside of them. Radar is an incredibly valuable tool for doing that."

Studying radar data to figure out whether what happened in Colorado was or wasn't a tornado is a perfect example. Radar helps dissect and measure a tornado's powerful mix of winds, rain, and energy to find the patterns that lead to tornadoes.

That's where the storm chasing comes in. It's how Robin collects the high-resolution radar scans. "We can see very small scales and detailed structures inside of the tornadoes," Robin says. But driving a radar truck toward supercells is

^ Radar is Robin's specialty. "Radar radiates microwave pulses out into the atmosphere," she says. "They backscatter off of precipitation particles and whatever else is out there and come back to us."

only part of it. "Doing the field work only takes about maybe a month out of every year."

What's she doing the other eleven months? "I'm sitting on my butt in front of the computer, analyzing the data, visualizing it, slicing and dicing it, and doing statistical analyses on it," says Robin.

She uses computers to visualize the tornadoes and the storms that made them.

Scientists have tornado-making computer software. "We can make an artificial storm on the computer," says Robin. You enter in the temperatures and humidity of a chunk of pretend atmosphere and hit *go*. "It'll grow and rise up, form

> Robin points out a line of storms on a radar map.

condensation [growing into a cloud], and become a storm based on equations." Weather by math!

A computer storm that makes a virtual tornado is interesting. But it's not real. That's where radar scans collected during storms help out. Robin loads her radar measurements into the computer. Then the software goes to work stitching the data together into a timeline of how the storm grew and made a twister. "We can use that to recreate the storm and test hypotheses about how it came into being," says Robin. Computer models learn from real-life examples, adding the knowledge to their program and getting smarter.

Robin can test the tornado computer model against the real thing, too. Like with what happened during the Greensburg, Kansas, tornado. Robin's team was storm chasing nearby on May 4, 2007, until their radar truck got a flat tire. While getting the tire replaced in Greensburg, a supercell thunderstorm started growing nearby. Might as well scan it, they decided.

"It was growing and growing and ended up dropping a wall cloud," remembers Robin. The supercell dropped a first tornado and then another. All eyes were glued to the radar screen when the big one happened. "It started producing this gigantic tornado signature."

Later, Robin put all the Greensburg radar data into the computer model and asked it to predict the tornado's path. It was dead on. The computer mapped out the same track the devastating tornado had taken through the town. "When I withheld the data from the mobile radar, the track and storm behavior wasn't nearly as accurate."

All that screen time and number crunching is the experiment that answers Robin's question about tornadoes or tornado behavior. "Once I come to a conclusion that's pretty clear, I can publish it in a scientific journal," says Robin. This is how the rest of the world learns about scientific discoveries. Robin writes a technical paper that describes the experiment, methods, and her conclusions. Then experts review it.

"It takes a really long time to get from collecting data in the field to actually publishing a paper on it—up to five years sometimes," says Robin. Good science takes time. Scientists want to make sure it's right before putting their name on it.

31

SHARING SCIENCE

During VORTEX2 Robin wrote up some of the tornado chases for the project's website. She liked it, so she decided to start her own blog. "I wanted people to have a glimpse inside the life of a research meteorologist," Robin says. And that includes storm chasing. "I would produce a blog post for every chase, explaining where I went and what I saw and I'd link to the videos or pictures of what was going on."

Why did she name her blog Tornatrix? She'd been trying to think up a name for both a blog and a Twitter handle. (Storm chasers are big on handles and call signs. It's a ham radio thing.) "I was kind of playing around with *tornado woman*, *twisteress*, that kind of thing," remembers Robin.

"And then *Tornatrix* popped into my head!" The word ending -*trix* means woman, like how aviatrix is an old-fashioned name for a female pilot. Perfect!

Robin's Tornatrix blog has been quiet the past few years. Time for blogging is hard to find these days between her job

< Robin and Dan teach meteorology at Purdue University.

and being a mom to two young sons. "But I do want to get back to it," says Robin. Her last blog post said goodbye to Oklahoma after thirteen years. She listed all the things she'd miss, including big tornadoes!

It was time to move on. Robin and Dan had jobs waiting at Purdue University in Indiana. Robin's radar skills would find new adventures there, including becoming a member of a new generation of VORTEX scientists. This one wasn't on the Great Plains. Its target? Dixie Alley.

Robin, Dan, and their boys, Dan Jr. and baby Paul. It's a busy life!

Tornado winds turn sticks into spears, shingles into scissors, and boards into battering rams.

Chapter 5
A Tragic Year

Eighth-grader Andrew Ellis looks like a linebacker. But the big fourteen-year-old is more than football tough. When Andrew was eight, an EF-4 tornado destroyed his grandmother's home while he was inside it.

The powerful 2011 twister killed everyone in the house except Andrew. His brother, cousin, grandmother, and great-grandmother all died. Only Andrew survived, and just barely. The tornado hurled the then-second-grader nearly a quarter of a mile (.4 km) from the ripped-apart mobile home. He lay unconscious and badly hurt in a cow pasture for hours until rescuers found him. Andrew doesn't recall being rescued, but he does remember the tornado.

35

The South was torn up by tornadoes in 2011. If you connected the destructive paths they took through the South end to end, they'd stretch farther than the width of the United States.

36

It happened outside Chattanooga, Tennessee. Andrew was watching TV at his grandmother's house that evening when the lights in the mobile home flickered. Then his cousin went to the window to see what was making the wind chimes go crazy.

A growing funnel cloud was speeding their way. Everyone rushed into the bathroom.

"I jumped in the bathtub, and my grandma jumped on top of me," Andrew said. Andrew remembers getting banged around in the tub and his grandmother being pulled away by the winds. "Then I'm like, flying in the sky," he said.

While in midair, Andrew saw swirling bits of house and branches. He was terrified of falling and landing on glass or shredded metal. "Then I fell face first into the ground," he said. "After I hit the ground, I don't remember anything."

The sun was rising by the time rescuers got Andrew to the hospital. His injuries were serious. One of his legs was badly broken. The winds of 190 miles per hour (306 kph) had dragged him over the debris-littered ground. The cuts all over his body were filled with glass, sticks, grass, and manure.

Andrew spent weeks in the hospital and months in rehabilitation. The eight-year-old had to learn to walk again. But with time and help, Andrew Ellis healed and grew into a healthy teenager.

"I was granted a fifty percent chance of living," Andrew said in 2017. "And now I've played football. I'm running around just being a kid." He knows that others weren't as lucky. In the Tennessee Valley alone, eighty people lost their lives on April 27, 2011, including the four generations of Andrew Ellis's family.

SOUTHERN SHOCKER

For three days, starting on April 25, 2011, tornadoes swarmed the South. Alabama, Arkansas, Georgia, Mississippi, and Tennessee all took multiple hits. When the chaos ended, 338 people were dead. Thousands more were injured.

An unimaginable 350 twisters spun down onto the ground during those seventy-two hours. April 27 was the worst day. Tornado warning after tornado warning was declared across the region during the outbreak.

TV meteorologists broadcast live for as many as ten hours straight, begging residents to take shelter as town after town lost power. Hundreds of giant electric transmission towers were toppled, power plants shut down, and parts of Huntsville, Alabama, were in the dark for days.

Some of the tornadoes were small and weak, but at least fifteen were EF-4s or EF-5s. These monster twisters crushed cars like pop cans. One threw

^ *The tornado that struck Trenton, Georgia, during the Super Outbreak of 2011 destroyed homes and knocked down tens of thousands of trees.*

^ *The Tuscaloosa tornado killed forty-four people on April 27, 2011. Its winds of 190 miles (310 km) per hour toppled even brick homes.*

an SUV into a water tower a mile away. A tornado-tossed photograph was found more than two hundred miles (322 km) from its destroyed home.

One of the EF-5s in Mississippi was so strong it ripped asphalt off a road, dug out two feet (61 cm) of dirt in places, and killed three people when it tossed their large mobile home three hundred yards (274 m) into a line of trees.

The 2011 Super Outbreak that ravaged Dixie Alley was a big deal for meteorologists, too. It topped the infamous Super Outbreak of 1974, when 150 tornadoes in thirteen states killed more than three hundred people. "We thought we'd never see another outbreak like it," Robin Tanamachi says. "And then the 2011 outbreak came along and turned out to be even bigger."

The staggering death toll shocked meteorologists. "How could this have happened with all of our technological advances, with all of our advanced understanding of how storms work?" asked Robin. "What went wrong?"

On a Sunday afternoon only three weeks later, it happened again. A mile-wide EF-5 tornado plowed through Joplin, Missouri.

Even with thirty minutes of warning time to take shelter, the tornado killed 158 people and injured more than a thousand. The Joplin twister's winds of 200 miles per hour (322 kph) ripped the town apart, destroying eight thousand homes, businesses, schools, and other buildings.

"The May 22, 2011 Joplin tornado was the first since 1953 to kill more than a hundred people," says Robin. "Up until then, we'd been patting ourselves on the back, saying there will never be a tornado that kills more than a hundred people ever again."

VORTEX2 had taught meteorologists a lot about how severe storms form tornadoes. "We thought we'd solved that problem." But in 2011, just a year after VORTEX2 ended, tornadoes killed 550 people in the United States.

"Mother nature came back and said, no, you didn't solve it. You still have a lot of stuff to work on," says Robin.

The tornadoes of 2011 did more than shatter homes and break hearts. Meteorological records were smashed, too.

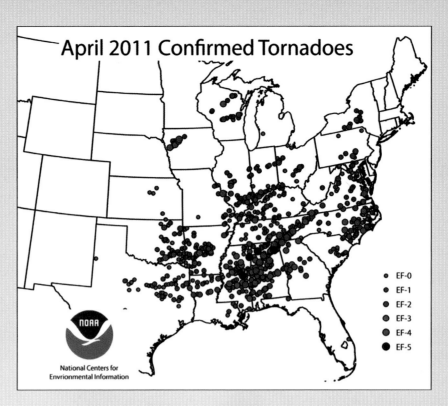

April 2011 Confirmed Tornadoes

- EF-0
- EF-1
- EF-2
- EF-3
- EF-4
- EF-5

NOAA

National Centers for
Envrionmental Information

< *The 2011 Super Outbreak hit Alabama hardest. The lives of 243 people were lost in the state.*

The powerful tornado that tore through Joplin, Missouri, in 2011 turned thousands of homes into piles of trash.

MOTIVATED BY DISASTER

To be fair, VORTEX2 didn't study tornadoes where the 2011 Super Outbreak
happened. "VORTEX2 was very focused
on the Central Great Plains region of the
United States," says Robin. "And for good
reason. That's where most tornadoes
happen." But the Great Plains isn't where
most *killer* tornadoes happen. They happen in Dixie Alley.

In an average year, seven people die
because of tornadoes in Oklahoma. In
comparison, Alabama and Tennessee
average thirty-eight deaths. That's nearly
five and a half times as many fatalities for
similarly sized regions.

The higher death toll is partly because more people live in Tennessee
and Alabama than in Oklahoma. But the
numbers still work out to twice as many
tornado deaths per capita in those Dixie
Alley states.

Why do Dixie Alley's twisters cause
so much misery and mess? What's differ-

< *Tornado expert Erik Rasmussen explains the
importance of VORTEX-SE to reporters.*

ent and so difficult about tornado tracking down South? Meteorologists aren't the only ones wondering. Government officials want answers, too. It's why VORTEX Southeast (SE) was created.

The mission of VORTEX-SE is to save lives through science and educate the public on how to stay safe. "Once we've learned about the storms, how they move and behave," Robin explains, "we need to figure out how people receive information and what affects their perception of how urgent or dangerous a situation is."

Knowledge doesn't help anyone unless it's put to use. "It's not all meteorology," adds Robin. It's understanding how people live, get information, and make decisions.

Heading up VORTEX-SE is Erik Rasmussen. He's studied tornadoes for the National Severe Storms Laboratory for more than twenty-five years. "This is the first VORTEX experiment to focus on tornado hazards as a whole," he says. "From the storms and conditions that produce tornadoes; to forecasting, detection, and warning; to the way communities and individuals receive and respond to those warnings."

Unlike the flat, wide-open Great Plains, the Southeast is hilly and covered in trees. Roads wind through hollows and wrap around ridges. Valley walls can act like a wind tunnel, shuttling wild wind gusts coming off a tornado down the valley ahead of the actual twister. Southern terrain likely affects tornadoes, says Erik. "But it also means you can't see a tornado until it's just a few seconds away from you. Which is a huge problem in trying to get to shelter." Especially for those living in mobile homes. These less sturdy houses are more common in the warm South.

"Not only do people not see it coming," agrees Robin, "but a lot of times they're in bed asleep."

Catching people off guard and unprepared is why nighttime tornadoes are more likely to kill. "Twenty-seven percent of tornadoes happen at night. But they're responsible for about thirty-nine percent of fatalities," says Robin.

Southern twisters aren't just springtime events either. Twisters touch down in winter there, too. Another reason they sometimes surprise folks.

Everything that makes southern tornadoes hard to spot makes them hard to study. It's not like the VORTEX experiments of the Great Plains, Erik says. "We could see those storms for thirty or forty miles [48–64 km] as they came at us. It was easy to set up instruments and make observations."

VORTEX-SE has to work differently. "In the southeastern US, with all the low clouds, haze, fog, trees and hills, it's going to be impossible to chase storms and catch tornadoes," Erik adds. Instead, they plan to set up a storm-snagging net of radar trucks, instruments, and scientists, "and just let the storms come at us and observe them as they move through."

Would it work? There was only one way to find out. Next stop: Huntsville, Alabama.

Chapter 6
Setting a Tornado Net

Where do scientists studying southern twisters meet up? The SWIRLL building at the University of Alabama in Huntsville. The home of the Severe Weather Institute and Radar & Lightning Laboratories, or SWIRLL, not only sounds tornado-ish, it looks it, too. The brick building wraps around a giant vortex-like spiraling staircase enclosed in a cone of glass.

Two dozen or so scientists crowd inside SWIRLL's impressive main control room for a late morning briefing. Out the windows is a partly sunny March sky. Some in the room grumble about the less-than-severe weather.

"It's the shear that's the problem," says a young man wearing a Mississippi State T-shirt.

ᵛ *The Severe Weather Institute and Radar & Lightning Laboratories (SWIRLL) building in Huntsville, Alabama.*

VORTEX-SE team members plan their attack.

^ Robin and the other VORTEX-SE team members check in on the weather.

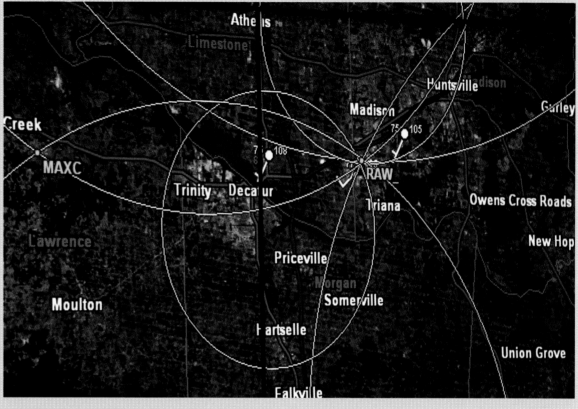

^ VORTEX-SE team members set their deployment area for the day.

"There's just not enough CAPE," a middle-aged woman adds. She's talking about convective available potential energy—CAPE—the stuff that fuels storms. Others chime in, complaining of weak low-level flow, disappointing dew points, and poor cellular convection.

"It's only 10:30," someone chimes in with a cheerful Texas twang. "Storms can still cook up."

Sunny skies are a bummer for this group. Everyone is hoping for bad weather—severe weather, actually. The kind that twists up tornadoes. It's what they've come from as far as Colorado and Massachusetts to study.

All eyes are on the massive nine-paneled screen that covers most of a wall. It shows a map of where Mississippi, Alabama, and Tennessee come together.

There are state borders marked in black, counties outlined in red, and highways drawn in yellow. There's also a fruit salad of differently sized icons, symbols, and numbers.

The map is difficult to read, much less understand. "It's complicated," agrees Robin Tanamachi. "That's why you go to college to learn this stuff."

Robin and the rest of VORTEX-SE are

^ *Robin discusses a close-up look of the rain on the radar map during the briefing.*

getting ready to set their tornado trap. All the map's symbols and numbers make up the knots of the net being laid. Once the teams of scientists drive off in their dozen or so different vehicles, this map will track where everyone goes and keep them updated. It's called SASSI, the Situational Awareness for Severe Storm Intercept.

SASSI is a computer program that shows all the collected weather information on a map. "In real time," notes Robin. Team leaders have SASSI on their laptops. This means that when they're out in the field they can watch the weather measurements coming in. And see where everyone else is.

Robin is in charge of one of three mobile radars during VORTEX-SE. Her team is using the X-Pol truck, the one whose radar looks like a giant metal mushroom. Its specialty? "Getting exceptionally high-resolution scans," says Robin. A detailed and up-close look inside a storm.

It's time to head out.

^ VORTEX-SE's weather maps include wind speeds, wind directions, and lines of barometric pressure.

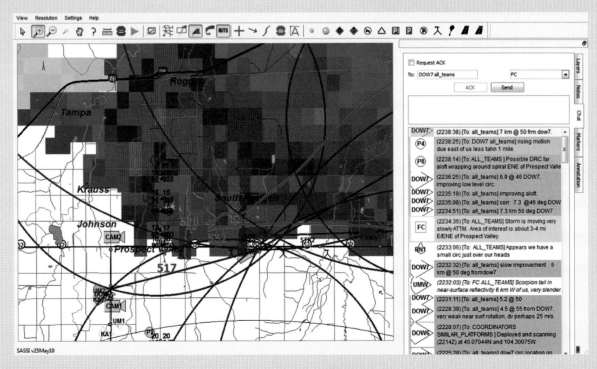

> VORTEX-SE uses a computer program called SASSI to communicate real-time weather information and show where teams are collecting data on a map.

BACK TO THE TRUCK

The radar truck exits the highway. It goes left at the top of the ramp, turning onto the overpass bridge. Down below, four lanes worth of traffic speed by on wet pavement.

By the time the radar truck is parked on the gravel shoulder, the sky looks more promising. Dark clouds clump and swell to the south. The rain has picked up and a stiff wind is pushing it sideways a bit. The lunchtime temperature is dropping, too.

Excellent. All are good signs of bad weather on the way.

Inside the cozy truck cab everyone's eyes are on screens.

Robin goes back and forth between watching her laptop screen of SASSI and X-Pol's incoming radar scans.

In the back, a meteorology student, Jessica Bozell, is sandwiched in next to a floor-to-roof stack of computer components, watching a mounted monitor.

^ Robin watches the radar data being collected in the truck cab.

47

Joe Waldinger, the radar's engineer from the University of Massachusetts, is keeping dry in the driver's seat. "I'm seeing some weird velocity things," he says, looking at radar scans. A gust of wind rocks the truck as if in agreement.

"Yeah, I see that," Robin answers, setting her laptop aside. "Let me get out and look at what we're dealing with here." As soon as she cracks open the truck door, wind and cold rain invade the cab.

Outside the sky is dark and the rain is like stinging pellets. Looking south, a thick bolt of blue-white lightning flashes. Unimpressed, Robin slams the door after climbing back in. Back to letting the radar look around.

"Now that's interesting," Robin comments after a bit, pointing to the radar scan on her laptop.

What's interesting? "This little comma shape." It's sort of a sloppy half swirl, like the last bit of bath water disappearing

down the drain. "That's what we call a mesoscale convective vortex." Vortex? As in a rotating vortex of wind—a tornado?

Nope, says Robin. A mesoscale convective vortex is simply a storm that pulls wind into a swirling shape. "It's a big weak rotation, rather than a nice tight rotation, like we would want to see with a tornado."

Switching to SASSI, Robin checks in to see where everyone else is. An icon that looks like a raindrop slides toward

Robin and her team hunker down in the truck, waiting for the storm to arrive.

Robin points out some stormy weather on the way.

^ *Robin gets ready to start scanning the skies.*

the comma-shaped storm. It's the vehicle Robin's husband, Dan Dawson, is in.

"Dan's racing, trying to catch up with this thing," she says. Robin hopes he's not the one driving. Raindrops hitting a windshield are a big distraction for Dan, she says. That's because raindrop shapes and sizes are what he studies.

SIZING RAINDROPS, PROFILING AIR

If you want to measure raindrops, a disdrometer is your tool. It sends a laser beam across a gap to a light sensor.

"When a raindrop, hailstone, or snow-flake falls through there, it breaks the beam up a little bit," says Dan, pointing to the instrument. Like a marble dropped in front of a flashlight beam, the instant of darkness created by a falling water droplet is recorded by the disdrometer.

By measuring the amount of laser light lost and for how long, the disdrometer figures out the kind and size of precipitation falling. Every ten seconds, the instrument records its findings. This way meteorologists like Dan can track the rate of rain over time. He's studying the disdrometer information from VOR-TEX-SE to see how it's different from raindrops in Tornado Alley.

"We want to compare them with storms on the Plains with higher CAPE," explained Dan. Raindrop size matters. Small drops evaporate faster than big ones. How much rain is falling and how many of those raindrops are changing into water vapor around storms makes a difference. Evaporation is cooling, like sweat leaving your skin. How many and how quickly raindrops evaporate during a storm affects whether it grows or dies. A lot of cooling robs a storm of heat, its fuel.

Dan Dawson sets up a PIPS, or Portable in Situ Precipitation Station.

^ *Dan checks on the PIPS's data recorder. After the storm, he'll download the information collected onto his laptop.*

Dan's disdrometer is mounted on what looks like a big heavy cube made of metal pipes. It's called PIPS—Portable in Situ Precipitation Station. Each PIPS has instruments to measure winds, temperature, atmospheric pressure, and humidity—as well as the laser disdrometer to measure the size of the raindrops.

Weather balloons are another tool VORTEX-SE uses to collect information. Each launched balloon carries a radiosonde more than 15 miles (24 km) up into the atmosphere. The radiosonde is a small package of weather instruments attached to a radio transmitter. It sends back measurements during its two-hour journey through the sky.

The radiosonde-collected temperature, pressure, humidity, and wind measurements are combined into a chart called a sounding. It shows meteorologists what the atmosphere is like at different heights from the ground up. Soundings are a big part of how CAPE is measured, and so very important for tornado scientists. Soundings are another part of the information net that goes into SASSI.

Dan gets the PIPS ready to record weather data. The disdrometer is the cylindrical stainless-steel instrument on the left. It measures the size of raindrops that fall in between its two halves.

51

VORTEX-SE scientists launch a weather balloon into the sky. The radiosonde is in the hand of the man on the left.

Back in Alabama, the storms are done for the day. The somewhat disappointed VORTEX-SE teams head for their hotels. Another meeting at SWIRLL is set for the next morning. They hope more bad weather will brew up overnight. If not, the teams will go home to Mississippi and Massachusetts, Tennessee and Texas, returning when the next round of severe weather starts up.

VORTEX-SE 2.0

Meteorologists continue to study the information VORTEX-SE teams collected in 2016 and 2017. "The project is ongoing," said Erik Rasmussen in late 2017. Scientists will go back to Huntsville to collect more data if the US Congress continues to fund the project. Science research costs money.

Thanks to VORTEX-SE, meteorologists are learning how southern tornadoes are different. "They are a lot less predictable than Great Plains tornadoes," says Erik. The storms that spin them out are harder to forecast, evolve more quickly, and move fast. They don't seem to need as much fuel, or CAPE, to get started, either.

The same facts that make Dixie Alley tornadoes different—and so deadly—make them hard to study. Surveying storms in VORTEX-SE turned out to be tough. Twisty country roads through woods and hollows make running down southern storms a challenge.

Laying a net of weather instruments that will catch a passing storm is a good plan. But it only works if you've picked the right trapping spot—at the right time. "We probably need to figure out how to cast a larger net," says Erik. Forecasting where the tornado-making storms will happen isn't easy. There's often more than one show going on at the same time. How to pick the winning one is a puzzle. "Even in northern Alabama, tornadoes are relatively rare," explains Erik. "We have to wait too long to sample enough storms to learn what we are after."

Robin agrees that Dixie Alley's tornadoes haven't given up their secrets yet. Collecting enough information to understand what's going on and draw conclusions will take time.

"We need at least five years," she says. Fortunately, she's got plenty of other work to do in the meantime.

^ StickNets are meteorological probes made for easy transport and setup. Each one measures and records barometric pressure, relative humidity, temperature, wind speed, and wind direction.

> PIPS includes the laser disdrometer (a), as well as a wind-speed-measuring anemometer (b), temperature-tracking thermometer (c), humidity-recording hygrometer (d), and a barometer (e) for assessing atmospheric pressure.

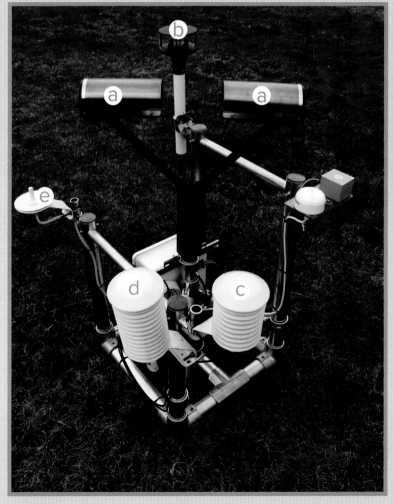

Storm clouds gather over Indiana farm country.

Chapter 7
Future Forecasts

The National Weather Service has issued a severe thunderstorm warning until five fifteen p.m. in the following Indiana counties . . . ," announces a computerized voice on the car radio. "Wind gusts can damage mobile homes and outbuildings. For your protection, move to an interior room . . ."

Robin Tanamachi turns off the car after pulling over on the side of a farm road. The air outside is warm and wet. It's late spring and the rain just stopped—for now.

A ceiling of steel-gray bubbling clouds stretches to the horizon. The sky is big here in Indiana farm country. Two teen boys fly past on ATVs, kicking up chunks of the dirt road that separates endless fields of evenly spaced stalks of young corn. The riders wear helmets, but no shirts. Neither seems much interested in the cars they just showered in dirt.

Robin is back on the chase. She's still after severe storms, though this time she's not in a radar truck. This warm afternoon, she and meteorology student Matt Seedorf are storm chasing for a different reason. Robin's testing some new equipment that could help get tornado warnings out faster.

> Robin gets the shortwave infrared
(SWIR) camera ready to go.

SEEING WITH SWIR

When the National Weather Service issues an official tornado warning, it means: take immediate action. It doesn't matter if you're making cookies, taking a shower, or playing baseball. Stop what you're doing. Find shelter.

Getting to shelter can take time, however. Some people need to get to a community building or a neighbor's basement. Students must file out of classrooms. Commuters in cars or buses have to get off the road. And you have to know there's a tornado warning before even heading to shelter. That's why warning time matters. The earlier the heads-up, the better. An extra minute can save lives.

"We're still looking to increase that warning time," says Robin.

Weather spotters are trying to help. These people are on the frontlines, constantly scanning the skies and reporting what they see. The National Weather Service has a network of radar domes all across the country. But radars can't scan every inch of the United States all the time.

Weather spotters help fill in the gaps by reporting tornadoes to the weather service. Robin is trying out a special kind of camera that could help spotters identify twisters. But to test it she needs to chase down some severe weather.

Luckily, they've already found some.

Ka-BOOM!

"Whoa!" says Matt. The clap of thunder is a chest thumper.

"That was probably a cloud-to-ground bolt over there," says Robin, pointing to a distant patch of dark sky that lightning just lit up. She goes back to fiddling with two cameras on opposite ends of a metal bar attached to a tripod. One is a regular video camera. The other is a special shortwave infrared (SWIR) camera. Instead of capturing regular video in visible light, the SWIR camera records in haze-penetrating infrared light.

Both cameras are running, filming the same patch of sky. The regular camera's screen shows a hazy gray sky over green fields topped with thick clouds.

The SWIR screen shows the same scene, but it looks pretty different. It's black and white and very sharp, like a high-def TV. You can pick out individual clouds in detail. Some look like towers, while others are oval-shaped globs.

"It's picking up the rain," says Robin, studying what the SWIR camera is showing on its screen. The rain is invisible to the regular video camera. Only SWIR sees it.

Bingo. It's working.

< Robin sets up the SWIR camera (left) next to a regular video camera so they can record simultaneously.

SPOTTER'S AID

The weather seems eager to please, so Robin and Matt drive closer to the storm. By the time they've set up the cameras again it's ten degrees colder. The storm is growing, sucking heat out of the air to fuel itself.

"That's a good-looking storm," says Matt.

The cameras record as Robin calls out its attractive features. "See the green tinge," Robin says, pointing to a gap in the thundercloud. "That's probably hail falling." Nice.

There's also a bowl-shaped bump growing on the bottom of the thunderstorm. Is it a wall cloud? The spot where tornadoes spin up before dropping down?

Nah. The bump isn't rotating. But it does look a bit like a wall cloud. Robin calls the cloud bump a fake-nado, a tornado lookalike. That's why Robin is filming it.

"I'd like to shoot it as a fake-nado example," explains Robin. It could help storm chasers and spotters learn the difference. That's what this chasing trip is all about. To find out if the SWIR camera sees what storm spotter eyes can't. "We're trying to get them another tool."

Let's say a severe thunderhead has a suspicious-looking lowering cloud. "But they can't see if it's rotating because it's locked in haze," explains Robin. Should a storm spotter (a) call in a tornado and trigger an official warning that sounds sirens, evacuates hospitals, and sends families to their basements? Or (b) not call in a tornado sighting yet, perhaps losing life-saving warning time if a twister does drop out and hit the ground?

The regular visible light (VIS) video camera (above) doesn't show the cloud details like the SWIR camera image (inset, right) does.

The SWIR camera could help decide between situations a and b. The camera cuts through the haze and gives a clearer picture of the storm—including whether or not there's a rotating wall cloud.

"The storm spotter would be able to report damaging or threatening weather to the weather service faster," says Robin. Faster means more warning time. And that saves lives.

^ Robin waits for the storm to roll in.

Robin adjusts the SWIR camera as the sky darkens.

TORNADO EVACUATION

The average time between a tornado warning and a tornado strike is thirteen minutes. If you learned about the warning right away, that's likely long enough to get to a neighbor's basement if necessary.

Extra time doesn't help people who don't know what to do, however. Or folks who ignore the warning.

The people in Joplin during the 2011 tornado had thirty minutes of warning time. But the twister still killed more than 150 people. Some people didn't take shelter when they heard the warnings.

Others waited to see if their particular neighborhoods were in harm's way. Less time means fewer options. Waiting till the last minute limits the kind of shelter you can get to. (Remember Andrew in the mobile home bathtub?)

Why would someone ignore a tornado warning? Because, chances are, a tornado will *not* strike. About three out of four tornado warnings are false alarms. Someone reported seeing a tornado or the radar showed what looked like a tornado being born—but no tornado strike happened.

A sign lets students know where to take shelter during a tornado.

TORNADO STORM SHELTER

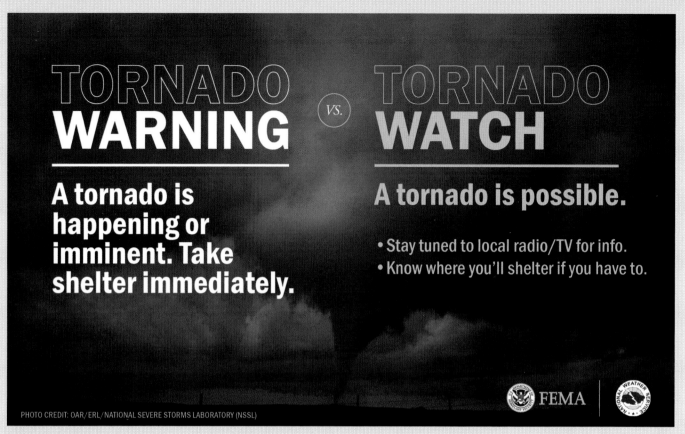

TORNADO
WARNING
VS.
TORNADO
WATCH

A tornado is happening or imminent. Take shelter immediately.

A tornado is possible.

• Stay tuned to local radio/TV for info.
• Know where you'll shelter if you have to.

FEMA

PHOTO CREDIT: OAR/ERL/NATIONAL SEVERE STORMS LABORATORY (NSSL)

^ *Part of staying safe during severe weather is understanding the differences between warnings and watches.*

Of course, chances are you won't get hit by a car crossing the street, either. But looking both ways and crossing at the crosswalk are still smart choices. It's just being safe.

Public officials want people to take severe weather warnings seriously. Improving warning time and reducing false alarms might help. The National Severe Storms Laboratory aims to do just that. "It's called Warn-on-Forecast," says Robin.

Warn-on-Forecast is an ongoing research project. Scientists are feeding tons of real weather information—radar, satellite, ground and air measurements—into powerful computer models. They hope to eventually create a computer system that will predict hazardous weather an hour ahead of time.

"We may actually reach a point where we can evacuate the path of the tornado," says Robin. It would be similar to how hurricane evacuations work now. People who lived where a tornado was likely to strike could leave ahead of the storm. Hospitals would have time to transfer patients. School buses could shuttle students away from oncoming danger.

It will take years to know if Warn-on-Forecast can work. There's a lot of data crunching and computer programing still to do. Local forecasters will need training to understand how to best use it to save

hile storm
anhandle.

Robin and her storm-chasing scientist colleagues gather information as safely as possible.

lives. When there are too many warnings, no one listens. Not enough warnings and no one takes action. Keeping people safe isn't simple or easy.

Meteorologists are at work on new storm-tracking instruments and better forecasting tools that can save lives. But improving public safety can require risk-ing personal safety—at least for torna-do-studying scientists! For now, seeing inside Earth's fastest windstorms means getting close to the action.

But don't get Robin wrong. "I am not an adrenaline junkie," she says. The only thrill she seeks is scientific discovery.

She does enjoy seeing huge storms and experiencing their intense power.

"I chase because I enjoy nature's majesty and spectacle," says Robin. It's all part of being a tornado scientist.

And that's all Robin Tanamachi ever wanted to be.

Words (and Acronyms!) to Know

air mass: large body of air with a uniform temperature and moisture

anemometer: an instrument for measuring wind speed

atmosphere: the blanket of air that surrounds Earth and lies between its land or oceans and outer space

atmospheric pressure: also called air pressure; the weight of the air from the ground (or water's surface) to the top of the atmosphere

CAPE: convective available potential energy; a storm's fuel

condensation: the process by which water vapor becomes a liquid; the opposite of evaporation

condensation funnel: the cone of cloud droplets that forms from a combination of the pressure drop inside a tornado and the ingestion of moist air

convection cell: a circular pattern of gas or liquid rising and falling as it's heated and cooled

disdrometer: a device for counting raindrop numbers and measuring their sizes

Dixie Alley: southern region of the United States where frequent destructive tornadoes occur; lower Mississippi River and Tennessee River valleys including much of Arkansas, Louisiana, Tennessee, Alabama, and Mississippi

Doppler radar: a type of radar that uses radio frequency changes to measure wind speed and direction

downdraft: a localized current of downward-moving air

evaporation: the process by which liquid water becomes water vapor

front: the boundary between two different air masses

funnel cloud: a rotating column of air that is not in contact with the ground

humidity: the amount of water vapor in the air

hurricane: a tropical cyclone on either side

of the Americas with winds of at least 74 miles per hour (119 kph)

hygrometer: an instrument that measures humidity

hypothesis: an idea or explanation for something that is based on known facts but has not yet been proven

mesocyclone: the column of vertically rising, spinning air inside a supercell thunderstorm

mesoscale convective vortex: A large rotating storm cluster, much larger than a supercell

meteorologist: a scientist who studies weather

NSSL: National Severe Storms Laboratory

NWS: National Weather Service

PIPS: Portable in Situ Precipitation Station

precipitation: water falling out of the air in either liquid (rain, drizzle) or solid (hail, snow) form

radar: short for radio detection and ranging; it's a technology for detecting distant objects like aircraft, but also detects rain, clouds, and storms

radiosonde: a package of weather-measuring instruments that travel through the air

rear flank downdraft: a strong downward flow of air on the backside of a supercell thunderstorm

SASSI: Situational Awareness for Severe Storm Intercept

severe thunderstorm: a thunderstorm with winds faster than 58 miles per hour (93 kph), hail larger than three-quarters of an inch (2 cm) across, or tornadoes

sounding: a set of weather measurements (temperature, humidity, pressure, winds, etc.) at a given time

supercell: a thunderstorm with a mesocyclone inside it

SWIRLL: Severe Weather Institute and Radar & Lightning Laboratories

tornado: a violently rotating column of air coming down from a thunderstorm cloud and in contact with the ground

Tornado Alley: central region of the United States where frequent destructive tornadoes occur; South Dakota, Nebraska, Kansas, Oklahoma, Texas

tropopause: the top boundary of the troposphere layer of the atmosphere

typhoon: a hurricane that forms in the northwest Pacific Ocean

updraft: a current of upward-moving air

vortex: spinning air (the plural is vortices)

VORTEX: Verification of the Origins of Rotation in Tornadoes Experiment

wall cloud: a lowered part of a thunderstorm cloud that sometimes spins and (more rarely) produces tornadoes

water vapor: the gas form of water

wedge tornado: a tornado that is at least as wide as it is tall

wind shear: the difference in wind speed and/or direction between two heights

^ Robin adjusts the SWIR camera as the sky darkens in 2001.

Find Out More

TWISTERS & TORNADOES

Fascinated by Earth's most violent wind-storms? Here are some websites to learn even more about them:

- The National Severe Storms Laboratory: www.nssl.noaa.gov/research/tornadoes
- Storm Prediction Center's Tornado FAQ: www.spc.noaa.gov/faq/tornado
- U.S. Tornadoes: www.ustornadoes.com

VORTEX SOUTHEAST

Check in on the Vortex Southeast team, read background information on the project, and watch their videos, too.

- www.nssl.noaa.gov/projects/vortexse

THE TORNATRIX

Read Robin Tanamachi's severe weather research blog for yourself!

- tornatrix.net

TORNADO SAFETY

Learn how to make a plan, be prepared, and stay safe during severe storms and tornadoes. These official US government websites tell you how:

- www.ready.gov/kids/know-the-facts /tornado
- www.cdc.gov/disasters/tornadoes/index .html
- www.ready.gov/tornadoes

ᵛ This cylindrical stainless-steel instrument is the disdrometer. It measures the size of raindrops that fall in between its two halves.

Robin poses for a perfect University of Wisconsin graduation day pic on the roof of the Atmospheric, Oceanic, and Space Sciences building.

Our Thanks!

A million billion thanks to Robin Tanamachi! Your willingness to participate made this book possible and your endless enthusiastic cooperation made it fun. You are a science rock star! We appreciate Dan Jr. and Paul sharing their mom with us. Our gratitude also goes out to the VORTEX-SE team members, chief among them Erik Rasmussen, for letting us sit in on meetings, tag along on balloon releases, ask endless questions, and generally be in the way. Our editor, Erica Zappy Wainer, deserves a shout-out, too. Thanks for making us a veteran SITF team.
—Tom & Mary Kay

69

Sources & Selected Bibliography

Quotes by Robin Tanamachi, Dan Dawson, and Erik Rasmussen were primarily gathered during in-person, email, and telephone interviews with the author. Other quotes and information sources are listed by chapter and topic below.

CHAPTER 2

July 18, 1986, Brooklyn Park, Minnesota, Tornado:

- "KARE News11 10pm Coverage of July 18, 1986 Fridley/Brooklyn Park Tornado." tcmedianow.com/kare-news11-10pm -coverage-of-july-18-1986-fridley brooklyn-park-tornado.

CHAPTER 3

May 31, 2013, El Reno, Oklahoma, Tornado:

- "2013 05 31 El Reno OK Tornado." Robin Tanamachi. YouTube video. www.youtube .com/watch?v=_TrguCGjXYs.

- The El Reno Survey Project. el-reno -survey.net.
- "May 31st, 2013 El Reno, OK Tornado." Dan Dawson. YouTube video. www.you tube.com/watch?v=07gEEMhWvXs.
- "The May 31–June 1, 2013 Tornado and Flash Flooding Event." National Weather Service. www.weather.gov/oun /events-20130531.
- Tornatrix blog. tornatrix.net/?p=1998.

Vortex2:

- "What is Vortex 2? Verification of the Origins of Rotation in Tornadoes Experiment 2." www.nssl.noaa.gov/projects /vortex2.

Tornado Science:

- Charlevoix, Donna J., Robert Rauber, and John Walsh. *Severe and Hazardous Weather: An Introduction to High Impact Meteorology*. Dubuque, IA: Kendall Hunt Publishing Company, 2014.
- Paul Markowski and Yvette Richardson,

"How to Make a Tornado," *Weatherwise* 66, no. 4 (July/August 2013): 12–18.

CHAPTER 4

Weather Radar:

- Tanamachi, R. L., H. B. Bluestein, M. Xue, W. Lee, K. A. Orzel, S. J. Frasier, and R. M. Wakimoto. "2013: Near-Surface Vortex Structure in a Tornado and in a Sub-Tornado-Strength Convective-Storm Vortex Observed by a Mobile, W-Band Radar during VORTEX2." Monthly Weather Review 141: 3661–90, doi.org /10.1175/MWR-D-12-00331.1.
- "Understanding Basic Tornadic Radar Signatures." February 14, 2013. www .ustornadoes.com/2013/02/14/under standing-basic-tornadic-radar-signatures.

May 4, 2007, Greensburg, Kansas, Tornado:

- "Megan Gardiner's Account of Surviving the Greensburg Tornado." *The Wichita Eagle*. April 29, 2009. www.kansas.com

/news/special-reports/article1006290.
html.

CHAPTER 5

April 2011 Tennessee Valley Tornadoes:

- "Boy Thrown Quarter-Mile by Tornado."
  Count on 2 First. June 9, 2011. www.nbc
  -2.com/story/14878907/2011/06/Thursday
  /boy-thrown-quarter-mile-by-tornado.
- Carroll, Chris. "Life, Death and Third
  Grade." *Chattanooga Times Free Press.*
  June 5, 2011. www.timesfreepress.com
  /news/news/story/2011/jun/05/life-death
  -and-third-grade/51241.
- Mitchell, Lori. "Tornado Survivor En-
  courages Others to Never Take Life for
  Granted." WRCBtv.com Chattanooga.
  April 27, 2017. www.wrcbtv.com/story
  /35271608/tornado-survivor-encourages
  -others-to-never-take-life-for-granted.
- National Oceanic and Atmospheric Ad-
  ministration. "Service Assessment: The
  Historic Tornadoes of April 2011." 2011.

www.weather.gov/media/publications/
assessments/historic_tornadoes.pdf.

CHAPTER 6

Vortex Southeast:

- "Bite-Sized Science: VORTEX Southeast." NOAAWP. February 29, 2016.
  www.youtube.com/watch?v=d2vSOh6
  jxZ0.
- Gentry, Phillip. "NOAA, UAH, and Part-
  ners Kick Off Tornado Study." March 2,
  2016. www.uah.edu/news/research
  /noaa-uah-and-partners-kick-off-tornado
  -study.

CHAPTER 7

Shortwave Infrared Camera Research:

- National Oceanic and Atmospheric
  Administration. "Weather Spotter's Field
  Guide." June 2011. www.weather.gov
  /media/owlie/SGJune6-11(1).pdf.

- Seedorf, Matthew, and R. Tanamachi.
  "Short Wavelength Infrared Imaging Im-
  pacts on Storm Spotting: A Pilot Study."
  November 10, 2016, American Meteorological Society Conference. ams.confex
  .com/ams/28SLS/webprogram/Manuscript
  /Paper301089/Matt%20Seedorf%20SWIR
  %20imagery%20Final%20Draft.pdf.

Warn-on-Forecast Program:

- National Oceanic and Atmospheric
  Administration, www.nssl.noaa.gov
  /projects/wof.
- Warn-on-Forecast Fact Sheet, www.nssl
  .noaa.gov/news/factsheets/WoF_2015
  .pdf.

^ Tornado scientist Howie Bluestein runs down a storm near Hollis, Oklahoma, in 2012.

Photo Credits

Index

75

SCIENTISTS IN THE FIELD

Where Science Meets Adventure

Check out these titles to meet more scientists who are out in the field—and contributing every day to our knowledge of the world around us:

  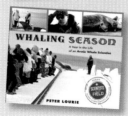   

Looking for even more adventure? Craving updates on the work of your favorite scientists, as well as in-depth video footage, audio, photography, and more? Then visit the Scientists in the Field website!

sciencemeetsadventure.com